365
Haiku

One Day at a Time

J G Lynn

Also by J G Lynn

Haiku From the Heart

Free Will in Machines:

    Essays on Intelligence and Consciousness

Forest Dragon Exercises I:

    An Introduction to Pai Lum Kung Fu for Health and Longevity

365
Haiku

One Day at a Time

J G Lynn

Nian Media

TM

www.NianMedia.online

TO PRINCESS KAREN

.

CONTENTS

Preface

In late 2018 I decided to start every day of 2019 by writing a haiku. This book is the result of that year long exercise.

Traditional Japanese haiku is a short form of poetry which consists of seventeen syllables in three phrases which consist of five, seven, and five syllables, for a total of seventeen syllables. The three phrases are traditionally written on three lines. The rhythm falls accordingly into the three phrases as in:

One two three four five

One two three four five six sev(en)

One two three four five

A haiku typically has a characteristic known as kiru, or cutting. The haiku will start by reflecting one thought and then "cut" to another, often pivoting on a single word or syllable. In modern times, especially outside of Japan, haiku is defined more loosely. It may have less than seventeen syllables and is often written on one line, three, or even in a circle. I have settled on my own interpretation of haiku as a form of poetry which is terse and concise, attempting to catch the essence of a feeling, mood, or situation while working within the structure of rules, often stretching them but not breaking them. I try not to hold too closely to the traditional rules of composing Haiku and instead have chosen to focus on expressing poignant and meaningful thoughts.

To me, haiku are about the connections we make with places, things, and our feelings. If you take the time to read one each day and meditate ponder, or just relax you will find that you too may make connections.

I hope these short bits of mental expedition will serve as inspiration to encourage you to begin each day pondering whatever is on your mind, wherever it may take you. The journal format of this book allows space at the bottom of each page to write some of your thoughts down.

– Write from the Heart –

J G Lynn

January 1

A new beginning,

awakening;

the future becoming the now.

Write from the Heart Write from the Heart Write from the Heart Write from the Heart Write from the Heart Write from the Heart

January 2

My soul is ready,

conquer the day; but sadly,

my body is not.

January 3

Sleepy, gray, blurry
– struggling to see;

a deep breath,
then slowly – I stand.

January 4

Peeking through the clouds,

the sun leans in;

it tells me my day has begun.

January 5

Sitting at the bar,

hearing the din –
through the crowd
I only see you.

Write from the Heart Write from the Heart Write from the Heart Write from the Heart Write from the Heart Write from the Heart

January 6

Sleeping through the day,

waking to eat –

it is good to be just a dog.

Write from the Heart Write from the Heart Write from the Heart Write from the Heart Write from the Heart Write from the Heart

January 7

Staring at the road

I see its cracks;

but I don't know where I

have been.

January 8

The woods are peaceful,

comforting me – offering

shelter from chaos.

Write from the Heart Write from the Heart Write from the Heart Write from the Heart Write from the Heart Write from the Heart

January 9

Blowing in the wind,

his regal mane dances to

the sound of his hooves.

January 10

Roaring through the trees,

like an angry old dragon

the cold wind stops me.

January 11

Burning deep within,

rising desire, urging me

to abide my fate.

Write from the Heart Write from the Heart Write from the Heart Write from the Heart Write from the Heart Write from the Heart

January 12

The birds have all flown

from winter's cold; I remain

and await their return.

Write from the Heart Write from the Heart Write from the Heart Write from the Heart Write from the Heart Write from the Heart

January 13

Flying down the hill,

wind in my eyes;

past the trees,

landing on my face.

January 14

Gazing on the pond,

mind like water; my soul comes

to rest in

my heart.

Write from the Heart Write from the Heart Write from the Heart Write from the Heart Write from the Heart Write from the Heart

January 15

Walking in darkness,

hearing only my footsteps,

I search for the light.

January 16

Inhaling the cold

moving slowly, pushing on;

waiting for the sun.

January 17

Sitting on the plane,

my eyes heavy; hope to sleep

and perchance – to dream.

Write from the Heart Write from the Heart Write from the Heart Write from the Heart Write from the Heart Write from the Heart

January 18

Snowflakes floating down,

cold breeze greeting; clouds parting,

sun shining, I smile

January 19

Darkness of morning,

peaceful, quiet;

foreboding,

   ahead of the storm.

Write from the Heart Write from the Heart Write from the Heart Write from the Heart Write from the Heart Write from the Heart

January 20

The wind is roaring

like a freight train; raging at

the house's windows.

January 21

Captured by winter's

white powder cloak, hid from sight

to return in spring.

Write from the Heart Write from the Heart Write from the Heart Write from the Heart Write from the Heart Write from the Heart

January 22

Coffee, very black,

before sunrise; warming hands,

along with my soul.

Write from the Heart Write from the Heart Write from the Heart Write from the Heart Write from the Heart Write from the Heart

January 23

Time to leave again,

sailing away; 'til I return

my heart remains with you.

Write from the Heart Write from the Heart Write from the Heart Write from the Heart Write from the Heart Write from the Heart

January 24

As the gentle rain

cools my body, gazing up

I now see heaven.

January 25

Staring into space,

peaceful and calm; …suddenly

I stand and walk home.

January 26

Forgetting the past

and the future, I find my

existence in life.

January 27

I lie in the woods,

a black bear prowls; stops briefly,

then lumbers away.

Write from the Heart Write from the Heart Write from the Heart Write from the Heart Write from the Heart Write from the Heart

January 28

Soft, thick, gray blanket

covers the sky; the bluebird

cocks his head then flies.

January 29

Snowflakes fall lightly

onto my face; clinging still,

there at rest I stand.

Write from the Heart Write from the Heart Write from the Heart Write from the Heart Write from the Heart Write from the Heart

January 30

White rabbit hopping

across the snow; suddenly

darts under a bush.

January 31

My heart beats wildly,

and breaths are short; waking up

… it's only a dream.

Write from the Heart Write from the Heart Write from the Heart Write from the Heart Write from the Heart Write from the Heart

February 1

The morning is cold,

the day stalks me; winding roads

provide my escape.

February 2

It's way too early,

my muscles say; they protest,

headed to the gym.

February 3

Dark, rich coffee beans –

grinding, brewing; in my cup,

nirvana is mine.

February 4

Birds will stay – singing,

but I will leave; my spirit

wanders to find home.

February 5

Buds on tree branches,

winter pauses; warmth erupts,

more cold yet to come.

February 6

Fog creeps gently in

across the pond; I wait for

the sun to appear.

Write from the Heart Write from the Heart Write from the Heart Write from the Heart Write from the Heart Write from the Heart

February 7

Crawling up the hill,

one thousand ants; their mission—

to bring home their lunch.

February 8

Reaching for the sky,

morning t'ai chi; I am ready

to approach the day.

February 9

Dark night closes in,

surrounding me; protecting

me from my worst fears.

February 10

Pondering the clouds,

seeing beyond; my eyes close,

slowly drift away.

Write from the Heart Write from the Heart Write from the Heart Write from the Heart Write from the Heart Write from the Heart

February 11

Up before sunrise,

way too early; headed south

to soak up the sun.

Write from the Heart Write from the Heart Write from the Heart Write from the Heart Write from the Heart Write from the Heart

February 12

Chasing the moonlight

across the sky; white dragons

devouring stardust.

February 13

Rain falls from the clouds

onto my face; morning air

chills me to the bone.

Write from the Heart Write from the Heart Write from the Heart Write from the Heart Write from the Heart Write from the Heart

February 14

Just before rising

to start the day, pull in close,

open up the heart.

February 15

Sleeping on the plane,

dreaming of home; the clouds part,

suddenly I wake.

February 16

Sitting in the dark

sipping coffee; keeping warm

until I wake up.

Write from the Heart Write from the Heart Write from the Heart Write from the Heart Write from the Heart Write from the Heart

February 17

Guarded by the trees,

deep purple clouds lie on the

horizon sleeping.

February 18

Sitting on the deck,

while power tools invade my

quiet peaceful world.

Write from the Heart Write from the Heart Write from the Heart Write from the Heart Write from the Heart Write from the Heart

February 19

Bowing to the day

with hands of peace; welcoming

all into my world.

Write from the Heart Write from the Heart Write from the Heart Write from the Heart Write from the Heart Write from the Heart

February 20

Standing and gazing

in the mirror; while slowly

becoming the void.

Write from the Heart Write from the Heart Write from the Heart Write from the Heart Write from the Heart Write from the Heart

February 21

Speeding through the night,

down the mountain; leaving the

sedated behind.

February 22

Diving deep beneath

the azure waves; destressing –

solitude at last.

Write from the Heart Write from the Heart Write from the Heart Write from the Heart Write from the Heart Write from the Heart

February 23

Sun rises early,

spring is coming; as the snow

slowly melts away.

February 24

Sleeping with the dogs

keeping me warm; one stretches,

one whimpers, one snores.

February 25

Standing in a field,

wind at my back; looking on

while the horse grazes.

February 26

Feet tired and dragging,

I climb the stairs – the lights dim,

my pillow beckons.

Write from the Heart Write from the Heart Write from the Heart Write from the Heart Write from the Heart Write from the Heart

February 27

Sitting in my chair

ruminating; I decide,

and the dog agrees.

Write from the Heart Write from the Heart Write from the Heart Write from the Heart Write from the Heart Write from the Heart

February 28

Into the darkness

soaring upward, leaving the

earth's ties far behind.

Write from the Heart Write from the Heart Write from the Heart Write from the Heart Write from the Heart Write from the Heart

March 1

A long, tiring day,

a long week ends; a short break,

ready for the next.

March 2

Up before the dawn

making pancakes; ten thousand —

done until next year.

March 3

A day without rain,

but cloudy skies; I'll just sit

at home and keep warm.

March 4

When will forever

come to an end; not too soon

or perhaps today.

March 5

The whole world at peace,

only a dream; but if so,

then let it be mine.

Write from the Heart Write from the Heart Write from the Heart Write from the Heart Write from the Heart Write from the Heart

March 6

End of a long day,

peace and quiet; contented

to lie in my bed.

Write from the Heart Write from the Heart Write from the Heart Write from the Heart Write from the Heart Write from the Heart

March 7

Sitting in the dark,

contemplating – what joys will

tomorrow bring me

March 8

Morning sun gleaming

across the snow; reflections

of the months gone by.

Write from the Heart Write from the Heart Write from the Heart Write from the Heart Write from the Heart Write from the Heart

March 9

The pig stares at me

and I smile back; we both pause

then go on our way.

March 10

Sick, lying in bed –

gazing outside; listlessly –

nothing left but sleep.

March 11

Dancing through the night,

beneath the stars; the trees and

the crickets join in.

Write from the Heart Write from the Heart Write from the Heart Write from the Heart Write from the Heart Write from the Heart

March 12

Stones under my feet

in the driveway; in stillness

hard and soft are one.

Write from the Heart Write from the Heart Write from the Heart Write from the Heart Write from the Heart Write from the Heart

March 13

Slicing through the air,

each advance free of thought,

at one with my sword.

March 14

My grumbling stomach

reminds my mouth – stop working

it is time to eat.

March 15

Running up the hill

chasing a deer; I stumble,

he quickly escapes.

Write from the Heart Write from the Heart Write from the Heart Write from the Heart Write from the Heart Write from the Heart

March 16

Lying in the tub,

absorbing heat; eagerly

waiting for healing.

Write from the Heart Write from the Heart Write from the Heart Write from the Heart Write from the Heart Write from the Heart

March 17

The road rises up,

wind at your back; warm sunshine

'til we meet again.

March 18

Snowflakes cling softly

on blades of grass; holding back

the coming of spring.

Write from the Heart Write from the Heart Write from the Heart Write from the Heart Write from the Heart Write from the Heart

March 19

Pulling the bow string,

my mind can see – the arrow

finding the target.

March 20

The train whistle blows

in the distance; while cloud veils

draw over the moon.

Write from the Heart Write from the Heart Write from the Heart Write from the Heart Write from the Heart Write from the Heart

March 21

Driving through the rain,

almost midnight; time to stop –

manhattans await.

March 22

Reclining in bed,

stomach grumbling; I reach for

my glass of Bordeaux.

Write from the Heart Write from the Heart Write from the Heart Write from the Heart Write from the Heart Write from the Heart

March 23

Dancing in the rain,

making a splash, and sliding

across the lanai.

Write from the Heart Write from the Heart Write from the Heart Write from the Heart Write from the Heart Write from the Heart

March 24

Twinkling stars at night

in a clear sky; carry me

far away from home.

March 25

Rich brown fields of earth,

cold on my feet; the stillness

surrounds me – at peace.

March 26

Troubled by the storm

building outside; remain calm

by looking inward.

Write from the Heart Write from the Heart Write from the Heart Write from the Heart Write from the Heart Write from the Heart

March 27

No haiku today,

too much to do; tomorrow

I'll have to do two.

Write from the Heart Write from the Heart Write from the Heart Write from the Heart Write from the Heart Write from the Heart

March 28

Sitting on the lawn

after sunset, the darkness

carries me away.

Write from the Heart Write from the Heart Write from the Heart Write from the Heart Write from the Heart Write from the Heart

March 29

Clouds of gray rolling

across the sky; bringing rain

over the desert.

March 30

Tapas afternoon,

cocktails at two;

continues

into the nighttime.

Write from the Heart Write from the Heart Write from the Heart Write from the Heart Write from the Heart Write from the Heart

March 31

Here in baggage claim

with the others; completely

at their mercy.

April 1

The first of April

only for fools? It depends

where you are standing.

Write from the Heart Write from the Heart Write from the Heart Write from the Heart Write from the Heart Write from the Heart

April 2

Enjoying the warmth

of April's sun; dreaming of

the summer to come.

April 3

A cold wind blowing

in from the field; a horse comes

and stands by my side.

Write from the Heart Write from the Heart Write from the Heart Write from the Heart Write from the Heart Write from the Heart

April 4

A roll of the dice,

flip of a coin; you never

know what to expect.

Write from the Heart Write from the Heart Write from the Heart Write from the Heart Write from the Heart Write from the Heart

94

April 5

Settling into night,

the clouds roll by; while musing on

my dreams to come.

Write from the Heart Write from the Heart Write from the Heart Write from the Heart Write from the Heart Write from the Heart

April 6

Thinking inside myself,

outside shut off; wandering

the labyrinth of my soul.

Write from the Heart Write from the Heart Write from the Heart Write from the Heart Write from the Heart Write from the Heart

April 7

The fog settles in

like a python; closing in,

constricting my mind.

Write from the Heart Write from the Heart Write from the Heart Write from the Heart Write from the Heart Write from the Heart

April 8

A large turkey crosses

the back lawn; finds his way

through the woods to the creek.

April 9

Clear skies up above

no clouds ahead; and the wind

gently helps me along.

April 10

After a full day

stillness feels good; my eyelids

grow heavy with sleep.

April 11

My senses heighten

with the night air; defined by

the steel of my sword.

April 12

Waiting for baby,

curled up inside; resisting

his grand debut.

April 13

On the patio,

the smell of smoke drifts through the

air into my nose.

Write from the Heart Write from the Heart Write from the Heart Write from the Heart Write from the Heart Write from the Heart

April 14

A tornado rips through

the villages; in its wake

lies only the past.

April 15

The little white dog

chases the turkey; which escapes

up into a tree.

April 16

Up with the sunrise,

no time to rest; scrambling to

stay ahead of the mob.

Write from the Heart Write from the Heart Write from the Heart Write from the Heart Write from the Heart Write from the Heart

April 17

The wind comes dancing

lightly across the water,

saltwater spraying.

Write from the Heart Write from the Heart Write from the Heart Write from the Heart Write from the Heart Write from the Heart

April 18

Striking out on the

long journey home; every step

carries me closer.

Write from the Heart Write from the Heart Write from the Heart Write from the Heart Write from the Heart Write from the Heart

108

April 19

Driving in the rain

the sky turns gray;

fog settles,

mist rises,

sun sets.

April 20

Springtime at the pond,

ducks congregate; discussing

the plan for the day.

Write from the Heart Write from the Heart Write from the Heart Write from the Heart Write from the Heart Write from the Heart

April 21

Our little dog lies

as she looks up; while resting

her chin on her bed.

April 22

Remnants of winter

lie on the lawn; scattered like

the rest of my life.

April 23

The day disappears

slowly over the horizon;

another day begins.

April 24

With the warm sunshine

of the morning, come the day's

opportunities.

April 25

A black ribbon slides

through the tall grass; disappears,

then attacks the mouse.

April 26

The creek rushes by,

    on through the trees;
collecting

         branches and
debris.

April 27

Rising from the ash,

the toves spiral; bringing back

memories of youth.

Write from the Heart Write from the Heart Write from the Heart Write from the Heart Write from the Heart Write from the Heart

April 28

The darkness creeps in

as the sun sets; and slowly

spreads into my heart.

April 29

Fog comes up slowly,

barely can see; then realize

it's only in my mind.

April 30

Walking through green grass,

feeling the cold on my feet,

dewdrops on my toes.

May 1

The path ahead lies

waiting for me; it goes on

'till the day I die.

May 2

Branches reaching out,

stretching upward; patiently

waiting for its demise.

May 3

The rain pours over

my body; soaking me,

it dissolves my stress.

May 4

I open my eyes

then smile and think – it's nice to

not wake up alone.

May 5

I awake to greet

a morning in paradise;

the way life should be.

Write from the Heart Write from the Heart Write from the Heart Write from the Heart Write from the Heart Write from the Heart

May 6

Walking through the park,

birds are chirping; on the way

to get some coffee.

May 7

Under the ocean,

beneath the waves, I dive down

to meet with an eel.

Write from the Heart Write from the Heart Write from the Heart Write from the Heart Write from the Heart Write from the Heart

May 8

Darkness rests over

the ocean's waves; bringing peace

after a long day.

May 9

Slowly the orange glow

creeps up over the hilltops

chasing off the night.

Write from the Heart Write from the Heart Write from the Heart Write from the Heart Write from the Heart Write from the Heart

May 10

The rain continues

another day; when will I

see the sun again?

May 11

Past the horizon

I cannot go; waiting to

see what comes to me.

Write from the Heart Write from the Heart Write from the Heart Write from the Heart Write from the Heart Write from the Heart

May 12

Bumblebees visit

as I daydream; wondering

how my days will end.

May 13

My excitement grows —

remembering — as my face

lights up like the sun.

Write from the Heart Write from the Heart Write from the Heart Write from the Heart Write from the Heart Write from the Heart

May 14

It's halfway through May

and still snowing; the wind blows

the cold from the North.

May 15

Gazing at the fields

through the window; nothing grows

except in my mind.

May 16

As the warmth returns

clouds disappear, revealing

the fire of the sun.

May 17

A cloak of darkness

slowly descends; putting birds

and creatures to bed.

May 18

Stars gaze down at me

and I stare back; searching for

a reason to live.

Write from the Heart Write from the Heart Write from the Heart Write from the Heart Write from the Heart Write from the Heart

May 19

Angry wind attacks

with great torrents mixed with hail,

then quickly passes.

May 20

The tree branches lie

across the lawn; the remnants

of last night's storm.

May 21

I roll out of bed,

struggle to stand – shaking the

cobwebs from my head.

May 22

When the rain comes down

the worms come out; the sun sends

them back to their homes.

May 23

The sound of gentle rain

on the rooftop brings me to

a gentle slumber.

May 24

As the sunlight sneaks

through the treetops, animals

wake to the new day.

May 25

All thoughts leave my head

as darkness falls; visions come

from another world.

May 26

Standing by the creek

bubbles float by;

escaping

the sins of

the mind.

May 27

Out on the golf course,

swinging my club; the geese make

great moving targets.

May 28

The humidity

wraps around me; like a wet

blanket on my skin.

May 29

Stumbling

...through the night

in the darkness,

finally,

I find my

way home.

Write from the Heart Write from the Heart Write from the Heart Write from the Heart Write from the Heart Write from the Heart

May 30

The river rises

over the bank;

a train calls

out in the distance.

May 31

Sitting in darkness

under the tree;

sipping on

evening fog,

. . . I sigh.

June 1

As the sun sinks low

the clouds turn blue; and the air

becomes filled with peace.

Write from the Heart Write from the Heart Write from the Heart Write from the Heart Write from the Heart Write from the Heart

June 2

Lazy afternoon,

nothing to do; tomorrow

is still far away.

Write from the Heart Write from the Heart Write from the Heart Write from the Heart Write from the Heart Write from the Heart

June 3

High in the mountain's

crisp morning air; solitude

and I are best friends.

June 4

A quiet morning,

nothing moves;

– except for the snakes and
spiders.

Write from the Heart Write from the Heart Write from the Heart Write from the Heart Write from the Heart Write from the Heart

June 5

I wake to dark gray clouds overhead;

. . . good morning to stay in my bed.

June 6

The sun rises high

over the trees; the grass stays

cool beneath my feet.

June 7

Sitting in the dark

as crickets chirp; day is done,

night begins, I sleep.

June 8

Sweating in the sun

the livelong day; make enough

just to stay alive.

Write from the Heart Write from the Heart Write from the Heart Write from the Heart Write from the Heart Write from the Heart

June 9

The smell of bacon

in the morning; memories

of last night's bourbon.

Write from the Heart Write from the Heart Write from the Heart Write from the Heart Write from the Heart Write from the Heart

June 10

Sipping foam from my

cappuccino; I ready

myself for the day.

Write from the Heart Write from the Heart Write from the Heart Write from the Heart Write from the Heart Write from the Heart

June 11

Each day I wake up

is a good one

– when I don't,

that may be
good too.

Write from the Heart Write from the Heart Write from the Heart Write from the Heart Write from the Heart Write from the Heart

June 12

Waking to a clear blue cloudless sky,

I see far into the future.

Write from the Heart Write from the Heart Write from the Heart Write from the Heart Write from the Heart Write from the Heart

June 13

Rain drips from the leaves

onto the ground; splattering

my plans for the day.

June 14

Walking down the path,

dogwoods in bloom; each new breath

begins life again.

Write from the Heart Write from the Heart Write from the Heart Write from the Heart Write from the Heart Write from the Heart

June 15

Walking down slowly

into the pond, where I am

greeted by two fish.

June 16

As my life goes by

I stop and think, how could it

ever be better?

June 17

Immortality

may soon be mine, if I can

stop living so fast.

Write from the Heart Write from the Heart Write from the Heart Write from the Heart Write from the Heart Write from the Heart

June 18

The end of the day,

I feel defeat; tomorrow

victory is mine.

Write from the Heart Write from the Heart Write from the Heart Write from the Heart Write from the Heart Write from the Heart

June 19

On a brighter day

I feel happy; but rainy

days are okay too.

Write from the Heart Write from the Heart Write from the Heart Write from the Heart Write from the Heart Write from the Heart

170

June 20

As the sky turns black

and the winds howl,

sheets of rain

come at me sideways.

Write from the Heart Write from the Heart Write from the Heart Write from the Heart Write from the Heart Write from the Heart

June 21

First day of summer,

cool mornings with longer days

and steamy hot nights.

June 22

Walking through the sand

to the water; followed by

a girl and her horse.

June 23

The evening star shines

through the darkness; as the night

replaces the day.

Write from the Heart Write from the Heart Write from the Heart Write from the Heart Write from the Heart Write from the Heart

June 24

Dark gray clouds of doubt

circle above; but I keep

my focus ahead.

June 25

Walking slowly up

the mountainside; at the top

lie fields of heather.

June 26

Sitting on the ground

looking upward – a breeze blows,

a bird sings, I smile.

Write from the Heart Write from the Heart Write from the Heart Write from the Heart Write from the Heart Write from the Heart

June 27

Sitting under the

starry night sky; can hardly

wait until morning.

June 28

Rain washes over

the young corn fields;

"be sure to

clean behind their ears."

June 29

Crickets are chirping

in the distance; farther yet

lies my heart's desire.

June 30

Summer erupts on

the last day of June;

as my soul

settles back and enjoys.

July 1

Walking along the

side of the road, two turtles

greet me as they pass.

July 2

First searing hot day

of the summer; plant leaves wilt,

dogs panting…I nap.

July 3

On the patio

contemplating the pebbles;

I can hear no one.

July 4

Independence Day,

what shall I do – a good time

to set my mind free.

Write from the Heart Write from the Heart Write from the Heart Write from the Heart Write from the Heart Write from the Heart

July 5

Clouds glide in front of

the red sunset; just before

the final curtain.

Write from the Heart Write from the Heart Write from the Heart Write from the Heart Write from the Heart Write from the Heart

July 6

Humidity hangs in

the cool night air, like cobwebs

that tangle my mind.

Write from the Heart Write from the Heart Write from the Heart Write from the Heart Write from the Heart Write from the Heart

July 7

Pink cotton candy

floats through the sky; imparting

sweetness to my soul.

Write from the Heart Write from the Heart Write from the Heart Write from the Heart Write from the Heart Write from the Heart

July 8

Sitting peacefully

in paradise; surrounded

by all of my friends.

Write from the Heart Write from the Heart Write from the Heart Write from the Heart Write from the Heart Write from the Heart

July 9

Far above the clouds

soars an eagle; free from the

limits of my mind.

July 10

Sipping an old wine

close to midnight, the future

becomes much clearer.

Write from the Heart Write from the Heart Write from the Heart Write from the Heart Write from the Heart Write from the Heart

July 11

When night comes early

I welcome her; succumbing

to dreams of rapture.

Write from the Heart Write from the Heart Write from the Heart Write from the Heart Write from the Heart Write from the Heart

July 12

The clouds slide across

the moonlit sky; I lean back

to breathe in the calm.

Write from the Heart Write from the Heart Write from the Heart Write from the Heart Write from the Heart Write from the Heart

July 13

Time melts around me

as I ponder what the day

might confront me with.

Write from the Heart Write from the Heart Write from the Heart Write from the Heart Write from the Heart Write from the Heart

July 14

A lone tree rises

in the pasture; it asks me

to rest in its shade.

July 15

The wind stirs the clouds

into
                    frenzied
                                    rain;

unleashing

                    merciless torrent.

July 16

Alone in my mind,

I hear echoes from
the past;

sadness fills my heart.

Write from the Heart Write from the Heart Write from the Heart Write from the Heart Write from the Heart Write from the Heart

July 17

Soft showers of rain

throughout the day; the evening

chases it away.

July 18

The sweltering heat

makes me lazy — like walking

home in a sauna.

July 19

Strolling aimlessly

deep in the woods; suddenly

I notice it's night.

July 20

Walking down the path,

no end in sight; no hurry,

enjoying the view.

Write from the Heart Write from the Heart Write from the Heart Write from the Heart Write from the Heart Write from the Heart

July 21

As morning goes by

the skies grow dark; lightning

brings glimpses of life.

July 22

The leaves sing like chimes

in the cool breeze; cicadas

drone in the distance.

Write from the Heart Write from the Heart Write from the Heart Write from the Heart Write from the Heart Write from the Heart

July 23

The sky is like a

clear blue lagoon; a small cloud

swims slowly past me.

July 24

Sitting by the stream,

falling asleep; a rabbit

stops to chat with me.

Write from the Heart Write from the Heart Write from the Heart Write from the Heart Write from the Heart Write from the Heart

July 25

Walking through the trees,

soft pine needles brush my face

so that I may see.

Write from the Heart Write from the Heart Write from the Heart Write from the Heart Write from the Heart Write from the Heart

July 26

Lying in the grass,

looking skyward, tomorrow

falling in on me.

Write from the Heart Write from the Heart Write from the Heart Write from the Heart Write from the Heart Write from the Heart

July 27

Worn out from the day

and chill of night; my eyelids

grow heavy…and close.

July 28

Headed down the road

into darkness; far ahead,

the future beckons.

July 29

As the steam rises

up from the pond, morning birds

call to their lovers.

July 30

Raindrops
dance
on
leaves
in the sunshine;

from a ledge,
a falcon watches.

Write from the Heart Write from the Heart Write from the Heart Write from the Heart Write from the Heart Write from the Heart

July 31

The red sky darkens,

clouds grow larger; preparing

for storms through the night.

August 1

Relaxing after

a long hard day; only sleep

matters to me now.

Write from the Heart Write from the Heart Write from the Heart Write from the Heart Write from the Heart Write from the Heart

August 2

Floating in the pool

after sundown; waiting for

another cocktail.

August 3

The sky is filled with

hot air balloons; like bubbles

at a great party.

August 4

The moon sinks lower

in the dawn sky,

to make room for a new

sunrise.

Write from the Heart Write from the Heart Write from the Heart Write from the Heart Write from the Heart Write from the Heart

August 5

Scant wisps of pink clouds

wander past me;

just maybe I could jump

on up.

August 6

The sky is crying

all around me; its warm tears

bring peace to my heart.

Write from the Heart Write from the Heart Write from the Heart Write from the Heart Write from the Heart Write from the Heart

August 7

The joy that I feel

as darkness comes; everyone

now at peace…restful.

Write from the Heart Write from the Heart Write from the Heart Write from the Heart Write from the Heart Write from the Heart

August 8

Crickets and tree frogs

sing me to sleep; 'till morning

I can be serene.

Write from the Heart Write from the Heart Write from the Heart Write from the Heart Write from the Heart Write from the Heart

August 9

My eyelids struggle

against the light; slowly I

rise to meet the day.

August 10

Hanging vines create

sanctuary; hiding from

curious neighbors.

Write from the Heart Write from the Heart Write from the Heart Write from the Heart Write from the Heart Write from the Heart

August 11

Nights getting cooler

and earlier; summer wanes,

soon will be…winter.

Write from the Heart Write from the Heart Write from the Heart Write from the Heart Write from the Heart Write from the Heart

August 12

Wasps build a large nest

under the eaves; buzzing like

party guests — the worst.

August 13

My senses recede,

joining my mind in the heart…

everything ceases.

August 14

Rows and rows of crops,

ready to serve as soldiers

in a food army.

August 15

Moonbeams light the clouds

from another dimension

as demons conspire.

Write from the Heart Write from the Heart Write from the Heart Write from the Heart Write from the Heart Write from the Heart

August 16

Driving cross country

for hours on end; gradually,

peace sets like sunset.

August 17

The sun burns brightly

against my skin; with no breeze

to offer relief.

Write from the Heart Write from the Heart Write from the Heart Write from the Heart Write from the Heart Write from the Heart

August 18

Raindrops fall gently

on the water; like children

playfully splashing.

Write from the Heart Write from the Heart Write from the Heart Write from the Heart Write from the Heart Write from the Heart

August 19

Swirling clouds of dust

dance across the field to the

music of the wind.

Write from the Heart Write from the Heart Write from the Heart Write from the Heart Write from the Heart Write from the Heart

August 20

Dark woods surround me,

lost in the gloom; with no guide

I look toward the moon.

August 21

Yawning as I rise,

out the window do I see

buffalo grazing?

Write from the Heart Write from the Heart Write from the Heart Write from the Heart Write from the Heart Write from the Heart

August 22

Walking at midnight

nowhere to rest; wandering

aimlessly 'til dawn.

August 23

The birds seem to know

what danger lurks; abruptly…

ominous silence.

Write from the Heart Write from the Heart Write from the Heart Write from the Heart Write from the Heart Write from the Heart

August 24

The mountain gazes down

onto the sea; enjoying

the waves on its feet.

Write from the Heart Write from the Heart Write from the Heart Write from the Heart Write from the Heart Write from the Heart

August 25

Before the rain begins

the clouds circle,

like vultures waiting for a feast.

Write from the Heart Write from the Heart Write from the Heart Write from the Heart Write from the Heart Write from the Heart

August 26

Between the tall trees,

wading through the long grasses,

trampling down the weeds.

August 27

A cool balmy night

in late August; puts my mind

to rest next to you.

August 28

The last bit of sky

turns from red to black and blue

along with my mood.

August 29

Darkness reaches deep

into my soul; exposing

my untold despair.

Write from the Heart Write from the Heart Write from the Heart Write from the Heart Write from the Heart Write from the Heart

August 30

Creatures great and small

languish at dusk; amid the

placid summer's edge.

August 31

Heaven above has

beautiful sky; below it

are all of my friends.

Write from the Heart Write from the Heart Write from the Heart Write from the Heart Write from the Heart Write from the Heart

September 1

September walks in

like an ogre; wrapped in a

dark blanket of fog.

September 2

Walking in circles

while the sun sets; what will I

do in the morning?

September 3

A woman's soft voice

reaches my ear, dulcet as

music in the wind.

September 4

Driving 'til midnight,

eyelids drooping; finally

I arrive at home.

Write from the Heart Write from the Heart Write from the Heart Write from the Heart Write from the Heart Write from the Heart

September 5

sitting home alone,

nobody here to talk with

except the crickets

Write from the Heart Write from the Heart Write from the Heart Write from the Heart Write from the Heart Write from the Heart

September 6

Live for the weekend,

only to find

that Monday

is not far behind.

Write from the Heart Write from the Heart Write from the Heart Write from the Heart Write from the Heart Write from the Heart

September 7

The distant moonlight

shines through cloudy skies like the

hope of forgotten dreams.

September 8

Creatures in the mist

emerge at dusk, as the stars

paint pictures above.

September 9

Endless walks at night,

listening to the owls calling

me in the distance.

September 10

The moon rises and

illuminates whole fields of

bright yellow flowers.

Write from the Heart Write from the Heart Write from the Heart Write from the Heart Write from the Heart Write from the Heart

September 11

Darkness quickly drops

over me like a cold blanket

over the hot fields.

September 12

Under the full moon

I see the love reflected

in your eyes…and smile.

Write from the Heart Write from the Heart Write from the Heart Write from the Heart Write from the Heart Write from the Heart

September 13

Early morning fog

keeps me in bed, while I wait

for the clouds to lift.

Write from the Heart Write from the Heart Write from the Heart Write from the Heart Write from the Heart Write from the Heart

September 14

Almost time for bed,

but my mind won't stop thinking of

everything I did.

September 15

Bells in the distance

reminding me to return

home and go to bed.

Write from the Heart Write from the Heart Write from the Heart Write from the Heart Write from the Heart Write from the Heart

September 16

Standing on the hill

watching over the valley,

away from the noise.

Write from the Heart Write from the Heart Write from the Heart Write from the Heart Write from the Heart Write from the Heart

September 17

Too many people

are making way too much noise

yet doing little.

September 18

Shivering in the

cold night air while sipping on

my glass of bourbon.

Write from the Heart Write from the Heart Write from the Heart Write from the Heart Write from the Heart Write from the Heart

September 19

Smoke drifts through the room,

people stumble by; I watch the

show from the corner.

Write from the Heart Write from the Heart Write from the Heart Write from the Heart Write from the Heart Write from the Heart

September 20

I stand looking up

at the treetops, as ashes

land on my eyelashes.

September 21

Nobody is near –

only the worms;

as the rain

calls out from the clouds.

September 22

In the pre-dawn mist

antlers appear with the crack

of oncoming footsteps.

September 23

Red sun reflected

in the windows; I can see

into the future.

Write from the Heart Write from the Heart Write from the Heart Write from the Heart Write from the Heart Write from the Heart

September 24

Dragging horse manure

across the yard; the horse just

wants to eat apples.

Write from the Heart Write from the Heart Write from the Heart Write from the Heart Write from the Heart Write from the Heart

September 25

Sitting in the dark,

one lone cricket telling me

I shouldn't worry.

September 26

Nothing in between

heaven and earth compares to

staying in bed late.

Write from the Heart Write from the Heart Write from the Heart Write from the Heart Write from the Heart Write from the Heart

September 27

A guitar playing

in the background; while the wind

whistles at the door.

September 28

Walking up the hill

to the last bar;

only to

find it has just closed.

September 29

Repeating the lies –

until the sheep

in ignorance

willingly believe.

September 30

Last of September

the sun shines bright;

attempting to hold back

the cold.

October 1

A majestic buck

emerges from the myst

to welcome me home.

Write from the Heart Write from the Heart Write from the Heart Write from the Heart Write from the Heart Write from the Heart

October 2

Buzzing from the crowd

becomes a vexation

to all our spirits.

Write from the Heart Write from the Heart Write from the Heart Write from the Heart Write from the Heart Write from the Heart

October 3

Better to be blessed

than be lucky; choose your path

or leave it to fate.

October 4

Clouds hang over me

impending doom,   'till the sun

rescues me from Hell.

Write from the Heart Write from the Heart Write from the Heart Write from the Heart Write from the Heart Write from the Heart

October 5

The nights grow colder

and days shorter; before long

the forest will sleep.

Write from the Heart Write from the Heart Write from the Heart Write from the Heart Write from the Heart Write from the Heart

October 6

I define my life

on my own terms; but the world

sets the conditions.

Write from the Heart Write from the Heart Write from the Heart Write from the Heart Write from the Heart Write from the Heart

October 7

An autumn morning

quiet and crisp, with gray clouds

keeping the sun at bay.

Write from the Heart Write from the Heart Write from the Heart Write from the Heart Write from the Heart Write from the Heart

October 8

A brisk wind catches

a falling leaf, taking it

away to its rest.

October 9

Too tired for haiku,

need to get sleep; everything

will keep 'till morning.

Write from the Heart Write from the Heart Write from the Heart Write from the Heart Write from the Heart Write from the Heart

October 10

Lying on its side

uprooted by the strong wind

a tree surrenders.

Write from the Heart Write from the Heart Write from the Heart Write from the Heart Write from the Heart Write from the Heart

October 11

As night falls it brings

our deepest fears; hope and faith

protect us 'til 'morn.

October 12

Up before the sun

ready to head out; dark again

when the day is through.

Write from the Heart Write from the Heart Write from the Heart Write from the Heart Write from the Heart Write from the Heart

October 13

Feeling lazy on

a cool gray morning; not a soul

disturbing the peace.

Write from the Heart Write from the Heart Write from the Heart Write from the Heart Write from the Heart Write from the Heart

October 14

A cold starlit night,

a cloudless sky; my mind is

as clear as the moon.

October 15

Ghosts appear to me

during the night; in daylight

they fade from my sight.

October 16

Winds howl through the night;

I stay sheltered in the house

hidden by darkness.

October 17

Above the chaos

stands one lone tree; leading the

way in rebellion.

Write from the Heart Write from the Heart Write from the Heart Write from the Heart Write from the Heart Write from the Heart

October 18

The morning sun shines

through the fall leaves; twixt the trees

I spot a small doe.

October 19

Falling to the ground

I can see the horse running

off in the distance.

Write from the Heart Write from the Heart Write from the Heart Write from the Heart Write from the Heart Write from the Heart

October 20

The sun has risen

high over the lake below,

the water glistens.

Write from the Heart Write from the Heart Write from the Heart Write from the Heart Write from the Heart Write from the Heart

October 21

Small white butterfly

flits in the sun . . . not knowing

when his life will end.

October 22

Splattering raindrops

on the windows, one million

dancing souls unite.

Write from the Heart Write from the Heart Write from the Heart Write from the Heart Write from the Heart Write from the Heart

October 23

Black caterpillar

with orange stripes says to me

winter is coming.

October 24

Machines ripping up

trees become a vexation

to peace of spirit.

Write from the Heart Write from the Heart Write from the Heart Write from the Heart Write from the Heart Write from the Heart

October 25

My ears become piqued
as darkness falls;
howling wolves
announcing the moon.

October 26

Lights nearby reflect

on the water, accented

by falling raindrops.

October 27

Dark clouds slowly part,

the sun pushes the blue sky

down over the earth.

Write from the Heart Write from the Heart Write from the Heart Write from the Heart Write from the Heart Write from the Heart

October 28

One star shines brightly

against velvet; as peace

descends on the earth.

October 29

Across the back lawn

leaves come crawling; attempting

to escape winter.

Write from the Heart Write from the Heart Write from the Heart Write from the Heart Write from the Heart Write from the Heart

October 30

Staring into space,

leaning backward in my chair;

surrounded by trees.

October 31

The cold autumn wind

howls through the streets,

and with it...

Halloween horror.

November 1

November arrives

riding on a cold, fast wind

followed by snow squalls.

November 2

The night sky is filled

with silvery clouds lit by a

sliver of the moon.

November 3

Behind the woodpile

I hear movement; as I turn

a rabbit runs by.

November 4

The red morning sky

warns me of storms I must face

the rest of the day.

November 5

The grass is still wet

from last night's rain; half asleep,

I walk to the pond.

November 6

Looking down, I see

a wasp struggle in the cold

to take its last steps.

Write from the Heart Write from the Heart Write from the Heart Write from the Heart Write from the Heart Write from the Heart

November 7

Death has a cold breath,

it follows me; I feel it

breathing down my neck.

November 8

I drag my feet through

the mud on the path to home …

only to find it gone.

November 9

The leaves fall forming

a red carpet, ushering

the winds of winter.

November 10

My heart freezes in

the falling snow; I dream of

better times to come.

November 11

Too many demands,

not enough time; my eyes shut,

I sleep to escape.

Write from the Heart Write from the Heart Write from the Heart Write from the Heart Write from the Heart Write from the Heart

November 12

White new fallen snow

helps brighten an otherwise

cloudy and gray day.

November 13

A deer crosses the road,

. . . he stops to look, to be sure

he lost the hunter.

November 14

As the night falls down,

peace settles in; coyotes

singing me to sleep.

November 15

Riding along past

the white fence posts, they guide me

home before sunset.

November 16

Small piles of snow melt

beneath the sun; overhead,

birds fly to the south.

November 17

Endless fields of brown

where corn once stood; harvested

to feed the cattle.

Write from the Heart Write from the Heart Write from the Heart Write from the Heart Write from the Heart Write from the Heart

November 18

Sitting in the tub

thinking of spring; my mind drifts

as bubbles float by.

Write from the Heart Write from the Heart Write from the Heart Write from the Heart Write from the Heart Write from the Heart

November 19

Fire on the mountain

lights up the night; a hint of

smoke drifts through the air.

November 20

Settling in to peace

and quiet; assisted

by a splash of gin.

Write from the Heart Write from the Heart Write from the Heart Write from the Heart Write from the Heart Write from the Heart

November 21

Standing at the door

waiting for you; and hoping

that no one is home.

Write from the Heart Write from the Heart Write from the Heart Write from the Heart Write from the Heart Write from the Heart

November 22

As night closes in

the day slows down; all too brief

'til the next gauntlet.

November 23

As the door opens,

the sun streams in, lighting up

the rest of the day.

Write from the Heart Write from the Heart Write from the Heart Write from the Heart Write from the Heart Write from the Heart

November 24

No stars in the sky;

Venus and Mars still shine on

the darkest of nights.

November 25

Silly little dog

walking around, room to room,

in search of the pack.

November 26

The pond's smooth surface

reflects my thoughts; the cold wind

whistles in my ear.

Write from the Heart Write from the Heart Write from the Heart Write from the Heart Write from the Heart Write from the Heart

November 27

I find I can fly

into the air through the clouds,

suddenly I awake.

November 28

Weight of the world

on my shoulders, I stand up

and take a deep breath.

November 29

A crop of brown grass

stands in the yard, defiant

against the winter.

Write from the Heart Write from the Heart Write from the Heart Write from the Heart Write from the Heart Write from the Heart

November 30

Standing in the breeze

watching the leaves floating down,

settling by my feet.

December 1

First of December,

sun sets too soon – and I brace

for a long winter.

December 2

After the rain stops

I walk outside through the fields

and wonder how long.

Write from the Heart Write from the Heart Write from the Heart Write from the Heart Write from the Heart Write from the Heart

December 3

White snowy powder

lies on the ground, just like a

sweet winter pastry.

Write from the Heart Write from the Heart Write from the Heart Write from the Heart Write from the Heart Write from the Heart

December 4

Hanging Christmas lights

in the tree,

wind and rain

help me work faster.

Write from the Heart Write from the Heart Write from the Heart Write from the Heart Write from the Heart Write from the Heart

December 5

Up and on the road

before the sun; another

sojourn to the east.

Write from the Heart Write from the Heart Write from the Heart Write from the Heart Write from the Heart Write from the Heart

December 6

Deep in the forest

as first light breaks, a buck stands,

poised, ready to run.

Write from the Heart Write from the Heart Write from the Heart Write from the Heart Write from the Heart Write from the Heart

December 7

Unable to move,

lying in bed; yesterday

was worse than I thought.

Write from the Heart Write from the Heart Write from the Heart Write from the Heart Write from the Heart Write from the Heart

December 8

White frost on the grass

glistens in the morning sun

then is quickly gone.

Write from the Heart Write from the Heart Write from the Heart Write from the Heart Write from the Heart Write from the Heart

December 9

Wind blows through the chimes

coaxing me as I struggle

to get out of bed.

Write from the Heart Write from the Heart Write from the Heart Write from the Heart Write from the Heart Write from the Heart

December 10

Winter settles in,

a sleeping bear, midway through

a wonderful life.

Write from the Heart Write from the Heart Write from the Heart Write from the Heart Write from the Heart Write from the Heart

December 11

Among the tall trees

stands a small oak;

unnoticed,

it escapes the axe.

Write from the Heart Write from the Heart Write from the Heart Write from the Heart Write from the Heart Write from the Heart

December 12

On the way back home,

riding for hours together,

we collapse in bed.

Write from the Heart Write from the Heart Write from the Heart Write from the Heart Write from the Heart Write from the Heart

December 13

Fog in the treetops

hangs over me; the sun glows,

chasing it away.

Write from the Heart Write from the Heart Write from the Heart Write from the Heart Write from the Heart Write from the Heart

December 14

Through the horse's eyes,

we ponder what to do and

the two of us agree.

Write from the Heart Write from the Heart Write from the Heart Write from the Heart Write from the Heart Write from the Heart

December 15

Ides of December,

beware the storm; the worst comes

always from within.

Write from the Heart Write from the Heart Write from the Heart Write from the Heart Write from the Heart Write from the Heart

December 16

Holidays are coming –

faster each day; but gone in

the blink of an eye.

December 17

My spirit floats free

from my body; only now

can I see myself.

Write from the Heart Write from the Heart Write from the Heart Write from the Heart Write from the Heart Write from the Heart

December 18

Rising through the air,

smoke from the fire reaches out

across the night sky.

Write from the Heart Write from the Heart Write from the Heart Write from the Heart Write from the Heart Write from the Heart

December 19

I look out over

snow dusted fields, immersed in

the depths of my soul.

Write from the Heart Write from the Heart Write from the Heart Write from the Heart Write from the Heart Write from the Heart

December 20

Waking up slowly,

my mind relives the events

of the night before.

December 21

The end of the day,

my back is sore and legs tired,

tomorrow – I'm done.

Write from the Heart Write from the Heart Write from the Heart Write from the Heart Write from the Heart Write from the Heart

December 22

Snow glistens on the

mountainside slopes, sculpted by

hundreds of skiers.

December 23

Orion is high

in winter's sky;

he chases

the seven sisters.

Write from the Heart Write from the Heart Write from the Heart Write from the Heart Write from the Heart Write from the Heart

December 24

Midnight Christmas Eve

all creatures speak; their message –

peace on Earth for all.

December 25

Air is crystal clear

stilled by the cold; motionless,

the woods are peaceful.

Write from the Heart Write from the Heart Write from the Heart Write from the Heart Write from the Heart Write from the Heart

December 26

Duke was eating hay,

briefly looked up, and then he

went back to eating.

Write from the Heart Write from the Heart Write from the Heart Write from the Heart Write from the Heart Write from the Heart

December 27

Standing arms outstretched

against the wind, leaning in –

my head back, eyes closed.

Write from the Heart Write from the Heart Write from the Heart Write from the Heart Write from the Heart Write from the Heart

December 28

Just after sunrise,
  sky of azure;
from a tree, a jay jeers
  at me.

December 29

Ice forms overnight
    across the creek;
mist rises
    as it starts to melt.

December 30

Up on the mountain,

walking on trails which lead to

views of the future.

December 31

In the final hours

of the best year ever yet —

until the next one.

Write from the Heart Write from the Heart Write from the Heart Write from the Heart Write from the Heart Write from the Heart

Next Year

Write from the Heart Write from the Heart Write from the Heart Write from the Heart Write from the Heart Write from the Heart

Write from the Heart Write from the Heart Write from the Heart Write from the Heart Write from the Heart Write from the Heart

Afterthoughts

Trying to write a haiku every day for one year without missing a single day was quite challenging. On some days it was very easy and a haiku just sprung into my mind, on other days it was real work just to come up with a theme. And on some days I would get to the end of the day and have nothing which meant I had to catch up at a later date. All in all it was enjoyable and I am glad I did this. But when I think about doing this for an entire year again, well… maybe someday.

Trivial Observations

In these 365 haiku the following words appear often.

The word *life* appears 9 times.

The word *home* appears 18 times.

The word *clouds* appears 35 times.

The word *morning* appears 24 times.

The word *night* appears 42 times.

The word *sky* appears 25 times.

The word 'til appears 10 times.